Hilary Koll and Steve Mills

Contents

		Introduction	2
Number	1	Counting (1) in 1s and 2s	4
	2	Counting (2) in 5s and 10s	5
	3	Odd and even numbers up to four digits	6
	4	Number patterns recognising and continuing	7
	5	Addition of numbers up to three digits	8
	6	Subtraction of numbers up to three digits	9
	7	Money writing prices correctly	10
	8	Money problems totalling prices	11
	9	Ordering and place value sequencing numbers	12
	10	Multiplication and tables learning multiples	13
	11	Division dividing and finding remainders	14
	12	Multiplication and division problems using real situations	15
	13	Fractions finding halves, quarters and three-quarters	16
	14	Test yourself: Test 1	17
Shape, space and measure	15	2D shape recognising and naming shapes	20
	16	Symmetry finding lines of symmetry and reflective symmetry	21
	17	3D shape recognising and naming shapes	22
	18	Right angles and turns recognising half, quarter and three-quarter turns	23
	19	Length measuring how long something is	24
	20	Mass and capacity using and reading scales	25
	21	Time telling the time; adding and subtracting time	26
	22	Data handling (1) using Venn and Carroll diagrams	27
	23	Data handling (2) reading a bar chart (block graph)	28
	24	Test yourself: Test 2	29
		Glossary	31
		Answers	31

Introduction

Key Stage 1 National Tests

Children between the ages of 5 and 7 (Years 1 and 2) study Key Stage 1 of the National Curriculum. Between January and June of their final year in Key Stage 1 (Year 2), all children take written National Tests (commonly known as SATs) in English and Mathematics. They also take part in tasks which are assessed as part of their classroom work. The tests and tasks are administered and marked by teachers in school. The test papers are also externally moderated to make sure that they are assessed consistently.

The tests and tasks help to show what your child has learned during Key Stage 1. In July the results will be reported to you and this will help you and your child's teacher to see whether your child is reaching national standards set out by the National Curriculum.

Understanding your child's level of achievement

The National Curriculum divides standards of performance in each subject into a number of levels, from 1 to 8. On average, children are expected to advance one level for every two years they are at school. By the end of Key Stage 1 (Year 2), your child should be at Level 2. If your child is working at Level 1, there will be some areas of Mathematics that they need help with. If your child is working at Level 3, they are doing very well, and are exceeding the targets for their age group.

The table shows how your child should progress through the levels at ages 7, 11 and 14 (the end of Key Stages 1, 2 and 3).

Key:
- ☐ Exceptional performance
- ■ Exceeded targets for age group
- ☐ Achieved targets for age group
- ▨ Working towards targets for age group

	7 years	11 years	14 years
level 8+			☐
level 8			■
level 7			■
level 6		☐	☐
level 5		■	☐
level 4	☐	☐	▨
level 3	■	▨	▨
level 2	☐	▨	▨
level 1	▨	▨	▨

The Test in Mathematics

The National Curriculum divides Mathematics at Key Stage 1 into three areas or Attainment Targets. These are 'Using and Applying Mathematics', which is assessed through classroom work, and 'Number' and 'Shape, Space and Measure' for which there is a written test.

This test begins with some oral questions and is followed by written questions. These contain a mixture of Number and Shape, Space and Measure questions, which the children are given the opportunity to attempt. Assistance is given with reading the questions and the test might be given in a small or large group setting. It may also take place in more than one sitting.

Levels of attainment

Once completed, the test is marked and a level and grade is calculated from the score. The level will be Level 1, 2 or in some cases 3. Level 2 is described as **a**, **b** or **c** and indicates whether the child has achieved a strong, middle or weak level. For example, **2a** means strong Level 2, and this tells you that your child is ready to begin Level 3 work at Key Stage 2. **2b** means a competent Level 2, but that there is still some Level 2 content to be learnt. **2c** means your child has achieved Level 2, but that your child is still some way from reaching the next level.

The Mathematics Test is intended to identify children working at Levels 1 to 3. This book is designed to assist children working at all three levels. Level 2, either **a**, **b** or **c**, is the expected level of attainment in Key Stage 1 National Tests. Children who achieve Level 3 with ease may be entered for the Key Stage 2 paper.

How this book will help

- This book provides the essential knowledge needed by your child to tackle the Mathematics Test with confidence.
- It revises work your child should be doing in class. It does not attempt to teach new material from scratch.
- The *Notes to parents* offer advice to enable you to work with your child, helping to improve understanding.
- The book gives practice in number skills, and covers the topics of Shape, Space and Measure to help your child prepare for the tests.
- The *Test Yourself* pages allow your child informal practice in the kinds of questions set in the National Tests.
- The answers on page 31 enable your child to learn from mistakes.

Using this book

When helping your child, remember the 'little and often' rule. Children working at Key Stage 1 are still quite young and may be tired after a demanding day at school. Make sure that the atmosphere is relaxed when you carry out the activities, and be ready to stop when you feel your child is becoming tired or frustrated. Above all, the activities in this book have been designed to provide a fun way of learning the skills and knowledge necessary for your child to produce the best possible work in the National Tests.

NUMBER

Counting (1)

This square shows the numbers up to 100 in lines of ten. This can help you to learn to count forwards and backwards in ones, in twos, in fives or in tens.

1	2	3	4	5	6	7	8	9	10
11	12	13	14	15	16	17	18	19	20
21	22	23	24	25	26	27	28	29	30
31	32	33	34	35	36	37	38	39	40
41	42	43	44	45	46	47	48	49	50
51	52	53	54	55	56	57	58	59	60
61	62	63	64	65	66	67	68	69	70
71	72	73	74	75	76	77	78	79	80
81	82	83	84	85	86	87	88	89	90
91	92	93	94	95	96	97	98	99	100

Counting in 1s

How far can you count? 1 2 3 4 5 6 7 8 9 10 ...

Can you count backwards? 40 39 38 37 36 35 ...

Counting in 2s

This pattern goes forwards in 2s: 2 4 6 8 10 12

You can start on a different number: 5 7 9 11 13

You can count backwards: 13 11 9 7 5

Activity

Practise counting forwards and backwards from different numbers.

76, 77, 78, 79 ...

Question

What are the next four numbers in these patterns?

22 24 26 __ __ __ __
21 19 17 __ __ __ __

Tip for parents

To help your child to practise the sequence of numbers 1–100, count your steps when walking together. Set limits: how many steps to the end of the road? the next tree?

Notes to parents

Counting forwards and backwards in different-sized steps is an important skill underpinning mental awareness of number. Give a number to begin on and ask your child to count on or back in ones, twos, fives and tens. The hundred square above can be used until your child can visualise the number patterns mentally.

2 Counting (2)

Counting in 10s

This pattern goes forwards in 10s: 10 20 30 40 50 ...

You can start on a different number: 3 13 23 33 43 ...

| When you count forwards in tens, the next number is always ten more. | T U
1 3
+ 1 0
2 3 | The unit digit stays the same. |

Counting in 5s

This pattern goes forwards in 5s: 5 10 15 20 25 30

You can count in 5s starting on a different number, like 2:

1 **2** 3 4 5 6 **7** 8 9 10 11 **12** 13 14 15 16 **17** 18 19 20 21 **22**

You can use this number line to count backwards in 5s from 22.

Can you see patterns in the numbers when you count in 5s from 2?

2 7 12 17 22 27 32 37 42 47...

Activity

Practise counting in tens from any number.

7, 17, 27, 37, ...

Question

What are the next four numbers in these patterns?

6 16 26 36 __ __ __ __

43 38 33 28 __ __ __ __

Tip for parents

Draw some number lines like the one on this page. Use them to help your child see different patterns.

Notes to parents

Counting forwards and backwards in different-sized steps involves seeing patterns in the numbers. For example, when counting in fives the same two units digits are repeated alternately, or when counting in twos beginning on an odd number, the other numbers in the sequence will also be odd. Discuss patterns such as these with your child.

3 Odd and even numbers

I'm the odd one out!

Even numbers are numbers that can be exactly divided by 2 with no remainder.

1   2   3   4   5   6   7   8   9   10

Even numbers: 2, 4, 6, 8, 10

The dots of these numbers can be grouped in pairs.

Odd numbers: 1, 3, 5, 7, 9

The dots of these numbers have one left over that cannot be paired.

Every whole number is either an odd or an even number. You can tell which it is by looking at the unit digit. Here the unit digit is underlined.

3<u>6</u>   6<u>5</u>   68<u>0</u>   23<u>4</u>   94<u>7</u>   194<u>1</u>

All even numbers end in **0, 2, 4, 6** and **8**.

All odd numbers end in **1, 3, 5, 7** and **9**.

3<u>6</u> 6 is even, so 36 is even.

6<u>5</u> 5 is odd, so 65 is odd.

Question

Are these numbers odd or even?

68<u>0</u>

94<u>7</u>

23<u>4</u>

194<u>1</u>

Tip for parents

Remind your child that odd numbers have an odd one out when arranged in pairs of dots.

Notes to parents

Ask your child to identify whether numbers are odd or even. Choose small and large numbers. Point out that the unit (or ones) digit shows whether a number is odd or even.

4 Number patterns

When you count in different-sized steps you make number patterns. These patterns can be continued by adding or subtracting the same number each time.

2 3 4 5 6   This pattern adds 1 each time.
2 4 6 8 10   This pattern adds 2 each time.
55 50 45 40   This pattern subtracts 5 each time.
86 76 66 56 46   This pattern subtracts 10 each time.

Activity
Make up some number patterns of your own. Write the first four numbers of each pattern. Give them to an adult to continue and to say what the pattern is for each one. Check the answers together.

Question

Find the next numbers in these patterns. Write what number is added or subtracted each time.

1 3 5 7 9 ___ ___ ___
This pattern adds ___ each time.

20 40 60 80 ___ ___ ___
This pattern adds ___ each time.

95 85 75 65 ___ ___ ___
This pattern subtracts ___ each time.

88 77 66 55 ___ ___ ___
This pattern subtracts ___ each time.

Notes to parents
Help your child to recognise patterns by finding the 'difference' between each number in the pattern.

or   86 76 66 56 46 36 26 16
        10 10 10 10 10 10 10

Once the difference has been found the pattern can be continued.

5 Addition

Addition is when we join together groups or numbers and find the total.

Here are some **addition** words:

| sum | plus | add | and |
| altogether | total | more | increase |

Add numbers in your head, if you can.

For **17 + 21** you might say: 17 + 20 + 1 = 38

Sometimes, with larger numbers, it is easier to write the sum down.

Remember to line up the hundreds, tens and units!

187 + 46 = 233

```
  H T U
  1 8 7
+   4 6
  2 3 3
```

Activity

Learn the numbers which add to make 10:
6 + 4,   7 + 3,
8 + 2,   9 + 1,
5 + 5.

Write the numbers between 0 and 10 all over a piece of paper. You can write each number more than once. Join any that add up to 10.

Question

Work out these in your head if you can:

57 + 19 =   73 + 27 =

Work out these on paper:

486 + 34 =   662 + 238 =

Tip for parents

Ask questions such as 'What is 3 add 6? double 7? 8 plus 7? 40 and 40?' Encourage your child to give the answers quickly. Use the range of addition words listed above.

Notes to parents

It is important for your child to memorise number facts. Simple calculations can then be done mentally, and will increase the speed and accuracy of your child's written calculations.

6 Subtraction

Subtraction is when we take away part of a group or number, or when we find the difference between two numbers.

Here are some **subtraction** words:

| take away | subtract | difference | less |
| minus | fewer | decrease | |

Subtract numbers in your head, if you can.

For **48 – 21** you might say: **48 – 20 – 1 = 27**

Sometimes, with larger numbers, it is easier to write the sum down.

Remember to line up the hundreds, tens and units!

183 – 47 = 136

```
  H T U
  1 8 3
-   4 7
  1 3 6
```

56 coins, take away 19 coins is ……

Question

Work out these in your head if you can:

85 – 51 =
77 – 22 =

Activity

Work these out on paper:

423 – 127 =
662 – 438 =

Tip for parents

When asking subtraction questions use the range of words listed above.

Notes to parents

When doing a calculation on paper, it does not matter if your child uses a different method from one you were taught yourself, provided that your child arrives at the correct answer. Speak to your child's teacher to find out the method your child has been taught.

7 Money

Know your coins!

10p

2p

1p

5p

20p

50p

You can use coins to practise making different **totals**, by adding, like this:

1p + 5p + 5p + 2p = 13p

Remember, you can't use numbers that are not real coins. You can't use 4p or 8p, for example.

£ is the symbol for **pound**. It is always put **before** the numbers.

p is the symbol for **pence**. It is always put **after** the numbers.

But the **£** sign and the **p** are never written together.

You can write **£1.49** or **149p**

Question

Which of the coins on this page do you need to make these totals?

18p
33p
76p
87p

Which of these is written wrongly?

£2.75p

275p

£2.75

Activity

Find the prices of things in the kitchen or of things in magazines. Read them out loud.

Tip for parents

Encourage your child to look at and read prices of items when out shopping. Ask what combinations of coins can be used to pay for them.

Notes to parents

Your child needs to become very familiar with the range of coins in our currency and the notation we use when writing prices on paper.

8 Money problems

When you use the £ sign, put a **decimal point** to separate the pounds from the pence:

£4.75   £3.05   £20.00

Three pounds and five pence is written as:

£3.05   not   ~~£3.5~~

The prices of these things can be written in two ways.

9p or £0.09

56p or £0.56

178p or £1.78

When adding prices which have pounds and pence, you must change them so that they are both in pounds or both in pence.

To work out £1.84 + 75p change to
either   £1.84 + £0.75 = £2.59
or   184p + 75p = 259p

Activity

 When you are shopping, try to work out the cost of two items or more. Practise writing the totals in pounds or in pence.

Question

Find the totals of these prices:

£7 + 84p =

£17 + 130p =

£1.64 + 50p =

34p + £12.60 =

Tip for parents

Playing shops is a good way for your child to practise writing prices and making totals.

Notes to parents

Many children have difficulty with writing amounts of money in £s because this involves decimals. It is important that they understand how to convert amounts given in pence to pounds.

9 Ordering and place value

Numbers between 9 and 99 are grouped in tens and units. **35** can be drawn like this:

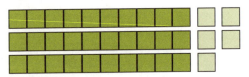

and can be written like this:

Thirty-five   **35**   **3** tens and **5** ones   **30 + 5**

Make sure you know how many tens there are in a number.

78 has **7** tens   **54** has **5** tens

Larger numbers have hundreds as well as tens and ones, like this:

534   has **5** hundreds, **3** tens and **4** ones
and can be written as **500 + 30 + 4**

We sometimes write HTU above the digits to help us.

H T U
5 3 4

When you put numbers in order of value, look at the hundreds first, then the tens then the ones.

121   **7**19   78   **5**75

The largest of these numbers is 719, because it has the most hundreds.

Activity
Write four large numbers on a piece of paper. Put them in order of value. Practise again with four more numbers.

Question
Put these numbers in order, the largest first.

44   18   163   67   5

Tip for parents
To practise ordering tens and units, collect up some stamps of different values under a pound. Ask your child to order them, the least first.

Notes to parents

Remind your child that, in any number, the left hand digit is the most significant because it shows how large the number is.

10 Multiplication and tables

Multiplication is a part of Mathematics where we use the sign ×. This is often called times and means 'lots of'.

3 × 4 means **3** lots of **4** = 12   **3 × 4 = 12**   * * * *
* * * *
* * * *

This is known as a times table fact.

It is important that you learn these times table facts.

Table of 2s
1 × 2 = 2
2 × 2 = 4
3 × 2 = 6
4 × 2 = 8
5 × 2 = 10
6 × 2 = 12
7 × 2 = 14
8 × 2 = 16
9 × 2 = 18
10 × 2 = 20

Table of 5s
1 × 5 = 5
2 × 5 = 10
3 × 5 = 15
4 × 5 = 20
5 × 5 = 25
6 × 5 = 30
7 × 5 = 35
8 × 5 = 40
9 × 5 = 45
10 × 5 = 50

Table of 10s
1 × 10 = 10
2 × 10 = 20
3 × 10 = 30
4 × 10 = 40
5 × 10 = 50
6 × 10 = 60
7 × 10 = 70
8 × 10 = 80
9 × 10 = 90
10 × 10 = 100

Did you know that if you turn a times table fact around, like this, you always get the same answer?

3 × 4 = 12   4 × 3 = 12

Question
Answer these tables facts.

5 × 2 =
2 × 5 =
7 × 10 =
10 × 7 =

Activity

Try turning around some tables facts of your own.

Notes to parents

If your child understands that tables facts can be turned around, the number of facts to be learned is halved! Help your child to become familiar with a range of words to do with multiplication, including multiply, times, multiplied by, product, lots of, groups of, double, twice.

11 Division

Division means splitting a number into equal-sized groups. We use this sign to show division ÷.

Here are some words to do with **division**.

| divide | divided by | share | shared between |
| half | quarter | remainder | |

This farmer has collected 24 eggs.

Her boxes hold 6 eggs each. How many boxes will she need to hold all the eggs?

We can write this as **24 ÷ 6**

Find out how many 6s are in 24: 6 + 6 + 6 + 6 = 24

There are 4 sixes in 24, so she will need 4 boxes.
24 ÷ 6 = 4 boxes

Sometimes the numbers don't divide exactly and so there are some left over. Any spare ones are known as the **remainder**, or just '**r**' so...
25 ÷ 6 = 4 r 1

Question

Answer these.

24 ÷ 4 =

24 ÷ 3 =

28 ÷ 7 =

25 ÷ 2 =

27 ÷ 4 =

24 ÷ 5 =

Tip for parents

When learning multiplication tables encourage your child to turn them into division facts.
For example, 3 × 5 = 15 becomes
15 ÷ 3 = 5 and
15 ÷ 5 = 3

Notes to parents

When asking division questions use the range of words listed above. When doing a calculation on paper, it does not matter if your child uses a different method from the one you were taught yourself, provided that your child arrives at the correct answer. Speak to your child's teacher to find out the method your child has been taught.

12 Multiplication and division problems

If the answer to a division question has a remainder, think what the remainder means. Always read the question carefully.

Look at this question.

> 180 children are going on a school trip on a coach. Each coach holds 50 children. How many coaches are needed?

This can be answered using division: **180 ÷ 50 =**

There are 3 lots of 50 in 180, so 150 children would fit into 3 coaches, with 30 left over.

180 ÷ 50 = 3 r 30

But the 30 left over are children. They need a coach so they can go too! So the answer here is **4 coaches.**

Question

140 children are going on a school trip on a coach. Each coach holds 25 children.

How many coaches are needed?

Activity

Write down a multiplication tables fact and then rewrite it as two division facts.

Notes to parents
Children often have difficulty with interpreting remainders in real situations where giving an answer with a remainder might not make sense of the question.

13 Fractions

If you split something into equal parts, you call each part a **fraction** of the whole thing.

Halves

Here is a pizza split into 2 equal pieces.

Each part is called a **half** and written as $\frac{1}{2}$ (**1** out of **2** equal pieces)

To find **half of a number,** split it into 2 equal parts. See how many are in one of those parts.

10 sweets in a packet

$\frac{1}{2}$ packet
5 sweets

$\frac{1}{2}$ packet
5 sweets

Quarters

Here is a pizza split into 4 equal pieces. Each part is called a **quarter** and written as $\frac{1}{4}$ (**1** out of **4** equal pieces).

Three-quarters is written as $\frac{3}{4}$ (**3** out of **4** equal pieces).

To find **a quarter of a number** split it into 4 equal parts. See how many are in one of those parts.

12 sweets in a packet

Question
Find a quarter of these numbers:

12	20
16	8
100	4
40	48
200	2

Activity
Learn the halves of these numbers:

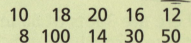

10 18 20 16 12
8 100 14 30 50

Tip for parents
Remind your child that a quarter can be found by finding half of a half.

$\frac{1}{4}$ packet — 3 sweets $\frac{1}{4}$ packet — 3 sweets
$\frac{1}{4}$ packet — 3 sweets $\frac{1}{4}$ packet — 3 sweets

---
Notes to parents
Fractions need to be discussed in context, in terms of half of something, with an emphasis on equal parts.

TEST YOURSELF

14 Test 1

1. Continue these patterns:
    a. 2   4   6   8   ....
    b. 97 87 77 67 ....
    c. 36 31 26 21 ....

2. What number is 10 more than each of these numbers?
   a. 67 ....   b. 95 ....   c. 136 ....   d. 690 ....

3. Write the numbers shown below:

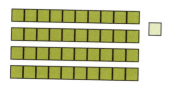  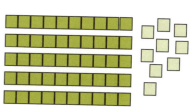

a. ....   b. ....   c. ....

4. Put these numbers in order with the smallest first.
   426   281   209   27   462   ....

5. If you need to, use paper to work out the answers.
   a. 67 + 22 = ...   b. 39 + 42 = ...   c. 76 + 18 = ...

6. Circle the odd numbers in the box below.

   15   107   168   192   760   371   663

Notes to parents

Parts 2, 3, and 4 require children to understand the value of digits in terms of whether they are worth hundreds, tens or units. Schools use practical equipment, as shown in part 3, to help children realise the relative size of digits in different columns.

Test 1 (continued)

7. If you need to, use paper to work out the answers.

   a. 67 – 22 =   **b.** 79 – 42 =   **c.** 56 – 27 =

8. Find the total of these coins:

Total = ...

9. How much change would you get from £1 if you bought these items?

 **a.** ....

 **b.** ....

10. Use two of these numbers to make 100

   25 50 10 75 4   ☐ × ☐ = 100

11. There are 26 children in a class. Half are girls.

   How many are boys? ....

12. Choose from these signs to make each answer correct.

   + – ÷ ×

   8 ☐ 2 = 16   8 ☐ 2 = 6   8 ☐ 2 = 4   8 ☐ 2 = 10

Notes to parents

Question 7 may highlight common errors, such as subtracting the smaller digit from the larger digit regardless of which is written on top. For example, children may answer incorrectly
    56
  – 27
    31

The use of practical objects can help children to realise that 7 cannot be subtracted from 6 without exchange. Ask your child's teacher for more information about the method of subtraction used at school.

Test 1 (continued)

13. Match each box to an answer with a line.

| 5 × 9 | 20 ÷ 5 | 10 × 7 | 6 × 5 | 50 ÷ 5 | 2 × 8 |

4   70   16
   18   45   10   30

14. There are 28 children in a class. The children get into pairs. How many pairs are there? ....

15. Colour in half of this shape.

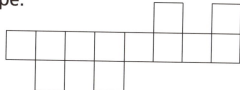

16. Colour in three-quarters of this shape.

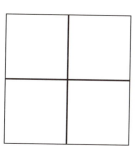

17. What is a half of these numbers?   **20** ....   **40** ....   **100** ....

18. What is a quarter of these numbers?   **20** ....   **40** ....   **100** ....

SHAPE, SPACE AND MEASURE

15 2D shape

2D shapes are flat shapes. You need to know the names of these shapes:

- A circle

Activity

Look around you. How many of these shapes can you see?

- A triangle has 3 straight sides.

- A rectangle has 4 right angles and 4 straight sides.

- A square has 4 right angles and 4 sides of equal length.

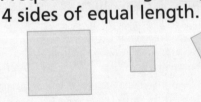

- A pentagon has 5 straight sides.

- A hexagon has 6 straight sides.

- An octagon has 8 straight sides.

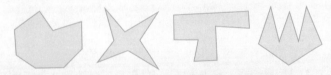

Notes to parents

Your child needs to learn the names and the properties of these shapes and understand that some of them, such as hexagons, can look very different from each other.

16 Symmetry

A shape has reflective symmetry when it has one or more lines of symmetry (mirror lines).
This flag has **2 lines of symmetry**.

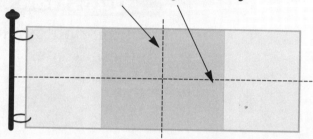

Imagine that this patterned tablecloth is folded along one of the lines. The two halves match! This makes the line a **line of symmetry**. This tablecloth has 4 lines of symmetry.

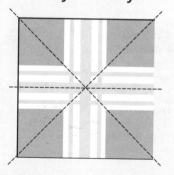

Question

Draw the reflection of this shape along the mirror line.

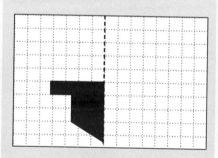

Activity

Fold a square of paper diagonally to make a triangle.

Fold it again ... and again.

Cut off the corners as shown.

Open out the shape. How many lines of symmetry does it have?

Tip for parents

Copy the flag and tablecloth shapes onto tracing paper. Let your child fold along the lines of symmetry to see how the two halves match.

Notes to parents

Help your child to position a mirror along the lines of symmetry in the diagrams above to see the reflected shape. Practising with the shapes first will help your child to answer the question on this page.

17 Right angles and turns

A **right angle** can also be called a **quarter turn**.

If the pointer is moved a **quarter turn**, it passes through one **right angle**.

We show a **right angle** by drawing a square close to where the arrows meet.

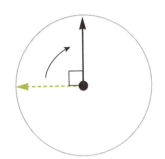

If the pointer is moved through 2 **right angles** we call this a **half turn**.

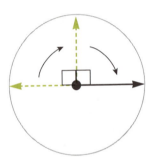

There are 4 **right angles** in a **complete turn**.

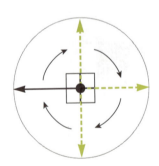

Activity
Look around the kitchen and find things that have right angles. Make a list of them.

Question
Tick the right angles in these shapes.

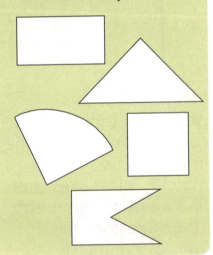

Tip for parents
To help your child recognise right-angled triangles, cut some out of paper, mix with triangles without right angles and arrange them in all directions on coloured paper. Ask your child to find the right-angled triangles.

Notes to parents

Your child may need some help to recognise right angles in shapes where the joining lines are not vertical and horizontal, as in some of the shapes in the Question on this page. Remind your child that a right angle is nothing to do with 'right' or 'left'. It can be at the top, at the bottom or in any direction!

18 3D shape

You can pick up 3D shapes, like cubes and cones. They have length, width and height.

Learn the names of these 3D shapes.

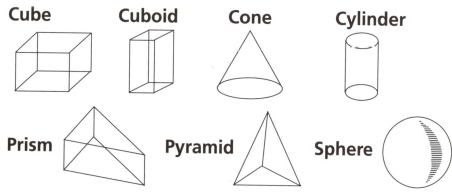

All these shapes have faces. Faces are the flat or curved surfaces on the shapes. A cube has 6 faces and a cylinder has 3 faces.

See how to sort these shapes into those with curved faces, those with flat faces and those with both.

A Venn diagram

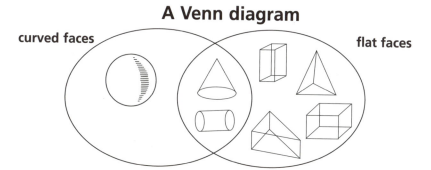

Activity

Look around your kitchen and see how many different 3D shapes you can find.

Question

Make a list of all the shapes in the Venn diagram and write down how many faces each one has.

Tip for parents

Remind your child that 3D shapes are sometimes called solid shapes.

Notes to parents

Your child needs to learn the names and the properties of these shapes and to realise that the faces of most 3D shapes are actually 2D shapes.

19 Length

To find out how long something is we measure its **length**. We can measure **length** in **centimetres** and **metres**. We can use a ruler to measure length, like this. This line is 9 cm long.

Use a ruler to measure these lines in centimetres.

These lines are not straight. Use string and a ruler to measure them, or **estimate** (make a good guess) then check with the string and ruler.

Activity

Choose some objects in your house and measure them. Choose some more and estimate the length. Use a ruler, and string if you need it, to check your estimate.

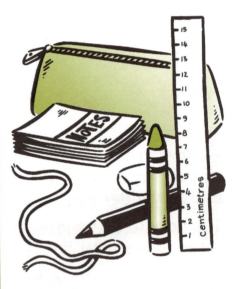

Question

There are 100 centimetres (cm) in a metre (m). How many centimetres are there in half a metre and in a quarter of a metre?

Tip for parents

Make measuring a game: both of you give length estimates for an object. Your child then measures the object. See whose guess is closest to the answer.

Notes to parents

Children often need help to measure accurately. Point out to your child that on some rulers, the 0 is a little way from the end of the ruler. Emphasise the importance of lining up the 0 with the beginning of the line being measured.

20 Mass and capacity

To find out how heavy something is we measure its **mass**.

We measure **mass** in **grams** and **kilograms**, using scales like the ones below.

Bathroom scales   Balance scales   Kitchen scales

This scale is showing 4 kg.

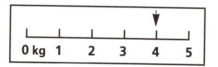

To find out how much something holds we measure its **capacity**. We measure **capacity** in **millilitres** and **litres**, using jugs and containers like the ones here.

Activity

Practise putting liquid into a measuring jug and reading the scale to find how much is in the jug.

Question

What measurements are these scales showing?

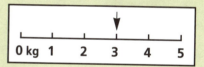

Tip for parents

Remind your child that there are 1000 grams (g) in a kilogram (kg).

There are 1000 millilitres (ml) in a litre (l).

Notes to parents

Children need plenty of practice in reading a variety of scales like the ones here. Mass is sometimes called weight.

21 Time

Time can be shown on clock faces and digital clocks. What times do these clocks show?

a.   b.   c.

On the first clock, count clockwise from 12 in fives up to the long hand. It's 30 minutes past the hour. Now look at the short hand. It's gone past 3. So the time is half past 3, or 3.30.
What times will the clocks show in half an hour?

Some of the clocks below show the same time. Can you see which they are? Draw lines matching them.

d.   e.   f.

g.   h.   i.

Activity
Practise telling the time on different clocks and watches.

Tip for parents
Remind your child that the long hand points to the minutes and the short hand to the hour. The hands move clockwise and there are 60 minutes in every hour.

Question
What time did each of the clock faces on the left show 20 minutes ago?

d:

e:

f:

Notes to parents
Ask children not only 'What time is it?' but also what time it was fifteen minutes or half an hour ago and how long is it until 5 o clock, etc.

22 Data handling (1)

We can use diagrams like the ones below to help us sort data. Here is a Venn diagram and a Carroll diagram.

Can you see how the shapes are sorted in both diagrams?

Venn diagram

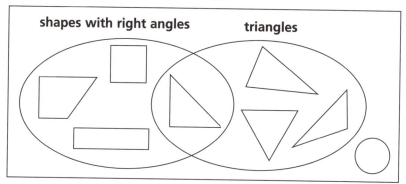

Carroll diagram

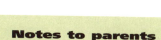

Activity

Use a Venn or a Carroll diagram to sort a pile of coins into circular coins and silver coins.

Question

Look at the diagrams. Which shape is not a triangle and has no right angles?

Notes to parents

To check a Venn diagram, trace your finger around one circle at a time. Check that everything in the circle has the named characteristic, e.g. the shapes have right angles, and that the elements outside do not have that characteristic. Check all circles in the Venn diagram in this way. The same can be done for Carroll diagrams, working horizontally and vertically along each row and column.

23 Data handling (2)

Some children have been asked to say what pets they have. Here are their answers:

cat dog gerbil gerbil fish gerbil
rabbit hamster cat dog fish cat
dog rabbit cat fish cat rabbit dog

We can show their answers like this:

pet	number of children
cat	5
fish	2
rabbit	3
hamster	1
dog	4
gerbil	3

Question

How many children own dogs?

How many children own rabbits?

This information can be shown in a **bar chart** or block graph, like this.

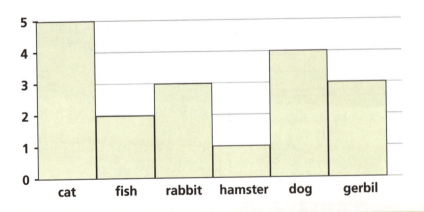

Activity

Draw a bar chart, using this information.

cat 2
dog 4
fish 3
rabbit 1

Notes to parents

The bars on a bar chart sometimes go across rather than up. Encourage your child to create bar charts using information about your home, family or favourite things.

TEST YOURSELF

24 Test 2

Answer the questions about these shapes.

a.   b.   c.   d.   e.

1. How many of the shapes are hexagons? ....

2. How many of the shapes are not hexagons? ....

3. How many of the shapes have a right angle inside? ....

4. Three of the shapes have reflective symmetry.
   Put a ✔ inside these three.

5. How much does this bucket hold? Join the right amount to the bucket.

   10 kilograms   10 metres   10 litres   10 centimetres

6. How heavy is this apple?   .... grams

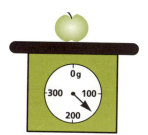

Test 2 (continued)

7. How long do you think this line is? Draw a ring around the best answer.

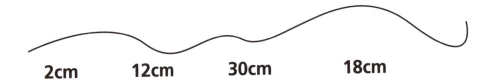

2cm   12cm   30cm   18cm

8. Measure these lines with a ruler:

………… cm   ………… cm

………… cm

9. Write in words the times these clocks show.

   6:30

....

7. What times will they show 45 minutes later?

....

Notes to parents

Telling the time is an important skill and involves more than reading a digital scale. It is necessary for children to understand the relationship of one time to another, for example, how far from 4 o'clock 3.35 is, and to realise that times can be presented in different ways.

GLOSSARY

addition (+)
(Page 8) joining together groups or numbers to make totals

bar chart
(Page 28) a way of showing data

capacity
(Page 25) how much something holds

Carroll diagram
(Page 27) a way of sorting data

data
(Page 27) information

decimal point
(Page 10) the dot which separates pounds and pence when writing prices

division (÷)
(Page 14) splitting a number into equal-sized groups

estimate
(Page 24) making a good guess at length, mass or capacity

even numbers
(Page 6) numbers ending in 0, 2, 4, 6, 8

fraction
(Page 16) a part of a whole; half, quarter, three-quarters

mass
(Page 25) how heavy something is

multiplication (×)
(Page 13) a number times another number: 3 × 4 = 12

odd numbers
(Page 6) numbers ending in 1, 3, 5, 7, 9

remainder
(Page 15) what is left over when one number has been divided by another number

right angle
(Page 23) a quarter turn

subtraction (−)
(Page 9) taking away part of a group or number to find the difference

symmetry
(Page 21) when a shape is the same on both sides of a line

2D shape
(Page 20) a flat shape

3D shape
(Page 22) a shape with length, width and height

ANSWERS

Answers to questions

Page 4
28 30 32 34
15 13 11 9

Page 5
46 56 66 76
23 18 13 8

Page 6
680 even
947 odd
234 even
1941 odd

Page 7
11 13 15 adds 2 each time
100 120 140 adds 20 each time
55 45 35 25 subtracts 10 each time
44 33 22 11 subtracts 11 each time

Page 8
76   100
520 900

Page 9
34   55
296 224

Page 10
10p + 5p + 2p + 1p = 18p
20p + 10p + 2p + 1p = 33p
50p + 20p + 5p + 1p = 76p
50p + 20p + 10p + 5p + 2p = 87p
£2.75p

Page 11
£7.84 or 784p
£18.30 or 1830p
£2.14 or 214p
£12.94 or 1294p

Page 12
163 67 44 18 5

Page 13
10
10
70
70

Page 14
6
8
4
12 r 1

6 r 3
4 r 4

Page 15
6 coaches

Page 16
3   5
4   2
25 1
10 12
50 ½

Page 21

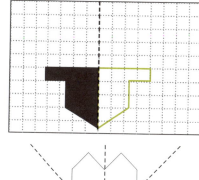

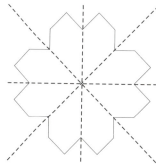

The shape has 4 lines of symmetry

Page 22

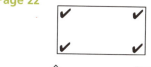

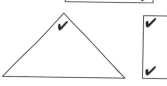

Page 23

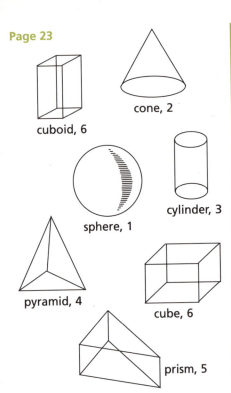

cuboid, 6
cone, 2
sphere, 1
cylinder, 3
pyramid, 4
cube, 6
prism, 5

Page 24
50 cms, 25 cms

Page 25
3 kg, 4.5 (4½) kg

Page 26
b quarter past 9   c quarter to 12

in half an hour:
a 4 o'clock   b quarter to 10
c quarter past 12

matching clocks:
d and i
e and g
f and h

20 minutes ago:
d 8.00
e 1.25
f 10.20

Page 27
the circle

Page 28
dogs: 4
rabbits: 3

Answers to tests

Test 1   Page 17

1. a. 10 12 14
   b. 57 47 37
   c. 16 11 6

2. a. 77
   b. 105
   c. 146
   d. 700

3. a. 41
   b. 45
   c. 59

4. 27 209 281 426 462

5. a. 89
   b. 81
   c. 94

6. 15 107 371 663

7. a. 45
   b. 37
   c. 29

8. 87p

9. a. 55p
   b. 63p

10. 4 × 25 or 25 × 4

11. 13

12. 8 × 2 = 16
    8 − 2 = 6
    8 ÷ 2 = 4
    8 + 2 = 10

13. 5 × 9 = 45   20 ÷ 5 = 4
    10 × 7 = 70   6 × 5 = 30
    50 ÷ 5 = 10   2 × 8 = 16

14. 14

15.

16.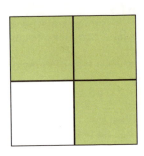

17. 10 20 50

18. 5 10 25

Test 2   Page 29

1. 2 (**b** and **e**)

2. 3 (**a**, **c** and **d**)

3. 2 (**a** and **b**)

4. **a**, **c**, and **e**

5. 10 litres

6. 150 grams

7. 12 cm

8. 7 cm, 9 cm, 5 cm

9. ten past four
   half past six or six thirty

10. five to five (or 4.55)
    quarter past seven (or 7:15)